Facts About the Gecko

By Lisa Strattin

© 2019 Lisa Strattin

Facts for Kids Picture Books by Lisa Strattin

Little Blue Penguin, Vol 92

Chipmunk, Vol 5

Frilled Lizard, Vol 39

Blue and Gold Macaw, Vol 13

Poison Dart Frogs, Vol 50

Blue Tarantula, Vol 115

African Elephants, Vol 8

Amur Leopard, Vol 89

Sabre Tooth Tiger, Vol 167

Baboon, Vol 174

Sign Up for New Release Emails Here

http://LisaStrattin.com/subscribe-here

Monthly Surprise Box

http://KidCraftsByLisa.com

Contents

INTRODUCTION

The gecko is a small to medium species of lizard that is found in the more temperate and tropical regions of the world. Geckos are commonly found around the Equator and in the Southern Hemisphere, although a few species of gecko are found north of the Equator in warm areas.

CHARACTERISTICS

There are thought to be over 2,000 different species of gecko found around the world. It is widely believed that there are more species of gecko that are not yet discovered. Geckos are found in a wide variety of colors and have many different markings on their bodies depending on the particular species.

They are well known for their ability to walk up vertical surfaces easily, even those as smooth as glass. Their feet are covered in tiny hairs that stick to surfaces just like sucker pads. This means that the gecko is a very agile animal.

APPEARANCE

The gecko is a lizard that comes in many colors and marking patterns. So, their descriptive trait is mainly, their size. With so many varieties, it is difficult to delineate except to note which lizard they are not. For example, they don't change color with their surroundings like the chameleon, they don't have an expanding frilled throat like the frilled lizard. It is easier to say what they don't look like than what they do.

They are found to be tan, brown, black, white, green, blue, orange, and yellow, with different styles of markings (spots, stripes and others) though all the different colors.

LIFE STAGES

After mating, the female gecko lays 2 sticky eggs, that have a soft shell and are white. The gecko eggs quickly harden so that the developing lizard inside is more protected. They do live a solitary existence. Although there may be many geckos around, they don't share their living space with others, in the wild.

The eggs of the gecko can take between 1 and 3 months to hatch because the incubation period depends on the species of gecko and the habitat in which it lives. The female gecko is not known to nurse or look after the baby geckos after they hatch. The babies are pretty much on their own when they hatch from the egg.

LIFE SPAN

Geckos have been known to live from 2 to 9 years.

SIZE

Geckos can range in size from just less than $1/10^{th}$ of an inch to 15 inches long and can weigh only 1/2 of an ounce. However, some can run as fast as 30 miles per hour!

HABITAT

Geckos are found in a variety of habitats in the warm parts of the world including: rocky deserts, mountains, jungles, rainforests, grasslands and even in urban areas where there are lots of people, where it is common to find geckos in people's homes.

DIET

Geckos are carnivorous reptiles so the diet is based on meat from other animals. Geckos primarily eat insects and worms, but some of the larger gecko species hunt small birds, reptiles and small mammals, like mice.

Some species of gecko are also known to eat a small amount of plants, like moss.

FRIENDS AND ENEMIES

Due to their small size, geckos have a number of natural predators around the world, with the snake being the biggest threat. Other animals that prey on the gecko include large spiders, birds and some mammal species.

SUITABILITY AS PETS

Today, many species of gecko are considered to be threatened with extinction due to habitat loss and pollution. Geckos are also popular pets around the world and many are caught in the wild to be sold into the exotic pet trade.

There are many common gecko varieties that are pets for people. They are easy to take care of and keep as pets. You can find out more about keeping a gecko as a pet from your local pet store or reptile shop.

COLOR ME

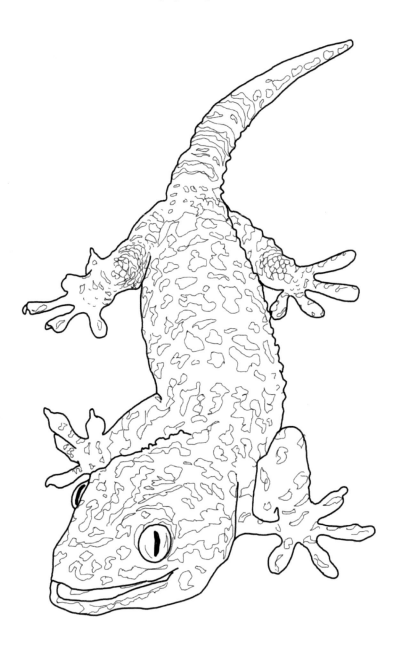

COLOR ME

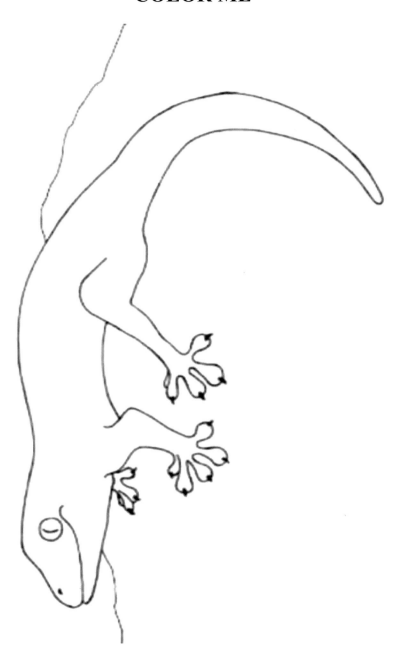

COLOR ME

COLOR ME

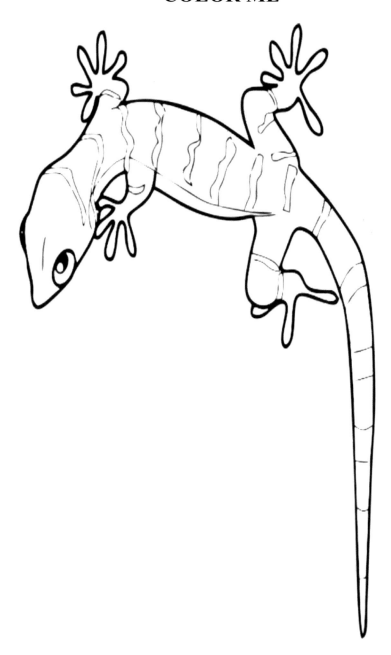

Please leave me a review here:

http://lisastrattin.com/Review-Vol-196

For more Kindle Downloads Visit Lisa Strattin Author Page on Amazon Author Central

http://amazon.com/author/lisastrattin

To see upcoming titles, visit my website at LisaStrattin.com– all books available on kindle!

http://lisastrattin.com

PLUSH GECKO TOY

You can get one by copying and pasting this link into your browser:

http://lisastrattin.com/PlushGecko

MONTHLY SURPRISE BOX

Get yours by copying and pasting this link into your browser

http://KidCraftsByLisa.com

Made in the USA
Monee, IL
08 March 2020